A MONTH of PRAYER WITH ST. THERESE of LISIEUX

A
MONTH
of PRAYER
WITH
ST. THERESE
of LISIEUX

CONTENTS

INTRODUCTION

Saint Therese of Lisieux (1873-1897)—also known as Therese of the Child Jesus and the Holy Face—lived a short life. She died at the age of twenty-four from consumption—what we now call tuberculosis. However, in her short life, she inspired many nuns in the Carmelite community of Lisieux, Normandy. She was canonized by Pope Pius XI in 1925 and wrote much regarding the path of humility and holiness befitting a Christian. She was acquainted with temptation and tribulation and learned to find joy in many sufferings. She was one of the most honored saints throughout the twentieth century, and her words still ring true today, inspiring Christians, young and old, who might hope to follow her path of piety.

DAY 1

We do not earn God's love any more than a child straight from the womb earns the love of their mother. God's love for His creatures is on account of that very fact—we are *his* creatures. Thus, St. Therese reflects on how God bestows His love on the simplest of us and the holy Doctors. He cares even for the "poor savage" just as much as He loves the refined and the wealthy. The basis of God's love is not in those whom He loves but in the character of His divine heart. Thus, we can take great comfort in how no matter our estate, our place in the world, our rank, or our past mistakes, God still "deigns to stoop" to our level and show us His love.

Meditations from St. Therese

The love of God reveals itself in the very simplest soul who resists His grace in nothing, as well as in the most sublime. Indeed, the characteristic of love being to humble itself, if all souls resembled those of the holy Doctors who have enlightened the Church, the good God would not seem to descend low enough in coming to them. But He has created the infant who knows nothing and can only wail; He has created the poor savage who has but the natural law for guidance, and it is even unto their hearts that He deigns to stoop.

HIST. D'UNE AME, CH. I

Additional Biblical Reflections: 1 Kings 8:23; Psalm 6:4; John 15:12-13.

Prayer

Lord, though we might be loved or unloved, welcomed or rejected, by the world, you are our maker and redeemer. We give thanks for your great love that considers not our worth, status, or merit, but only the merits of Christ in whom we are all adopted as your beloved children. Let us draw nearer to you in your love that we might within your embrace demonstrate your unwavering love to one another. Amen.

DAY 2

The path of holiness is not complicated. All the rites, prayers, and practices embraced by the saints boil down to a basic but fundamental Biblical principle—love. However, to say that the path of holiness is *simple* does not mean that it is easy. The demonstration of God's love, through Jesus, was simple, but the journey to the cross was arduous and costly. To follow the saints' path does not require a special insight or revelation, but rather, a heart willing to follow the path of the cross, the path of love.

Meditations from St. Therese

I know of one means only by which to attain to perfection: LOVE. Let us love, since our heart is made for nothing else. Sometimes I seek another word to express Love, but in this land of exile the word which begins and ends is quite incapable of rendering the vibrations of the soul; we must then adhere to this simple and only word: TO LOVE. But on whom shall our poor heart lavish its love? Who shall be found that is great enough to be the recipient of its treasures? Will a human being know how to comprehend them, and above all will he be able to repay? There exists but one Being capable of comprehending love; it is Jesus; He alone can give us back infinitely more than we shall ever give to Him.

LETTER TO HER COUSIN MARIE GUÉRIN

Additional Biblical Reflections: Micah 7:18; 1 Corinthians 13:13; Luke 9:23.

Prayer

Lord, the path toward intimacy with you was revealed to us clearly. Yet, too often, we resist the path of love. Soften our hearts, Lord, and give us the endurance and willingness to take up our crosses in the image of your Son's love for the world that we, too, might offer ourselves to as living sacrifices. Amen.

DAY 3

God is liberal in His love. However, embracing His love requires self-surrender and gratitude. It is not enough to surrender ourselves to His love while imagining we are entitled to it. Gratitude and thanksgiving are more than good manners. It is how we take hold of God's love and embrace it not as something we merit but as a gift merited only by Christ on our behalf.

Meditations from St. Therese

Oh! if souls weak and imperfect as mine, felt what I feel, not one would despair of reaching the summit of the mountain of Love, since Jesus does not demand from us great deeds, but only self-surrender and gratitude. I have no need, saith He, of the goats of thy flocks . . . If I were hungry I would not tell thee . . . Offer unto God the sacrifice of praise and thanksgiving. See then, all that Jesus asks of us! He has not need of our works but only of our love. This very God who declares that He needs not to tell us if He were hungry, did not hesitate to beg of the Samaritan woman a little water . . . He thirsted!!! But in saying: "Give me to drink," it was the love of His poor creature that the Creator of the universe besought. He thirsted for Love! And now, more than ever is Jesus athirst. He meets with none but the ungrateful and the indifferent among the disciples of the world; and amongst His own

5

disciples He finds, alas! very few hearts that surrender themselves without any reserve to the tenderness of His infinite Love.

HIST. D'UNE AME, CH. XI

Additional Biblical Reflections: 1 Chronicles 16:8; Psalm 49; John 4:7.

Prayer

Lord, all things we have come to us out of your open heart. Engender within us hearts of gratitude that we might not boast of our status as your children but cherish every good gift that comes from your hand. Amen.

DAY 4

We are people who have been given much. We have even been given callings. This pattern of having received takes new shape in the form of charity as we serve others through the callings and tasks the Lord has given us in love. Thus. St. Therese reminds us that love "comprises all vocations," and no matter how humble a work we might do, whether it be serving kings and presidents or waiting on tables, in all things we are called to serve.

Meditations from St. Therese

Charity gave me the key to my vocation. I understood that the Church being a body composed of different members, the most essential, the most noble of all the organs would not be wanting to her; I understood that the Church has a heart and that this heart is burning with love; that it is love alone which makes the members work, that if love were to die away apostles would no longer preach the Gospel, martyrs would refuse to shed their blood. I understood that love comprises all vocations, that love is everything, that it embraces all times and all places because it is eternal!

HIST. D'UNE AME, CH. XI

Additional Biblical Reflections: Proverbs 19:13; Luke 21:1-4; 1 John 3:17.

Prayer

Lord, if anyone ever had reason to boast, it was you. Still, you humbled yourself to dwell among us—even accepting a death befitting a common criminal in our place. Let us not boast of our status and rights but, rather, let us live lives that consider others first, lives shaped by charity. Amen.

DAY 5

One of the temptations that can befall us when we are charitable is that we begin to take credit and pride in our benevolence. We might also be tempted to judge those who appear less virtuous than us. However, St. Therese reminds us that even when we act in a godly way, it is on account of Jesus who acts through us. Because it is Jesus who works through us, we know that Jesus is the one who works—and is constantly working—through our fellow believers. Thus, there is no room for pride. It is the same Lord who works through us all.

Meditations from St. Therese

I feel that when I am charitable it is Jesus alone who acts in me; the more I am united to Him the more do I love all my Sisters. If, when I desire to increase this love in my heart, the demon tries to set before my eyes the faults of one or other of the Sisters, I hasten to call to mind her virtues, her good desires; I say to myself that if I have seen her fall once, she may well have gained many victories which she conceals through humility; and that even what appears to me a fault may in truth be an act of virtue by reason of the intention.

HIST. D'UNE AME, CH. IX

Additional Biblical Reflections: Colossians 3:12-14; Roman 7:17-20; Philippians 2:1-5.

Prayer

Lord, every move we make is on account of you and your Spirit, who dwells in us. Let us not grow prideful in our virtue that your goodness might become an occasion for vice. Rather, let us celebrate the ways you choose to work through others and give thanks for however you have chosen to work in our hearts. Amen.

DAY 6

Today's meditation is brief but profound. While we are to be mindful of the company we keep—that we not be lured into sin—we are also called to humble ourselves, love our enemies, and do as Jesus did when he ate with sinners, much to the chagrin of the Pharisees. When we only seek company with those we like, it is ultimately a symptom of our pride—we are using those with whom we keep company to satisfy our own needs, our desire for companionship that satisfies our emotions, and the like. When we seek the companies of even those whom we do not particularly like or appreciate, the Lord can open our eyes to see past our shallow judgments and demonstrate that on account of Christ, we are all one body and members of His church.

Meditations from St. Therese

I ought to seek the company of those Sisters who according to nature please me least. I ought to fulfil in their regard the office of the Good Samaritan. A word, a kindly smile, will often suffice to gladden a wounded and sorrowful heart.

HIST. D'UNE AME, CH. X

Additional Biblical Reflections: 1 Corinthians 5:11; Mark 2:13-17; Luke 15:7.

Prayer

Lord, while we are called out of the world and should not keep unsavory company, we are also called to embrace the lowly and rejected. Let us not be prideful about the company we keep but give us hearts for the outcasts and the despised that we might be ever mindful of the fact that we, too, were outcasts and despised on account of our sin when Jesus came to die for us. Amen.

DAY 7

In today's meditation, St. Therese addresses Jesus's controversial teaching that he should gladly give the cloak off his back if one comes to contend with him. In our world, we become quite attached to our property and material goods. But here, St. Therese reminds us that, for our Lord, the reward of being a servant to others is greater than that of any material benefit. Rather than asking how I can protect what is mine, she suggests, the question one should ask is how I can render service to others with all that God has given me.

Meditations from St. Therese

Oh! what peace inundates the soul when she rises above natural sentiment. No joy can compare with that known to one who is truly poor in spirit. If he ask with detachment for some necessary thing, and it is not only refused him, but an attempt made besides to deprive him of what he already has, he follows the counsel of our Lord: "And if a man will contend with thee in judgment and take away thy coat, let go thy cloak also unto him." To yield up our cloak means, I think, to renounce our last rights, to consider oneself as the servant, the slave of others. When we have abandoned our mantle it is easier to walk, to run; therefore Jesus adds: "And whosoever will force thee one mile, go with him other two." It is not enough that I should give to whosoever may ask of me, I must forestall their desires, and show that I feel much gratified, much honored in rendering service; and if they take a thing that I use, I must seem as though glad to be relieved of it.

HIST. D'UNE AME, CH. IX

Additional Biblical Reflections: Proverbs 19:17; Matthew 5:40-42; Luke 3:10-11.

Prayer

You are both Lord and servant of all. While you rule over the earth, you also open your hand to satisfy all your creatures' needs. Grant us hearts for service that we might find more gratification in giving unto others than in acquiring material goods and wealth. Amen.

DAY 8

St. Therese here observes that, particularly for his close friends and family, Jesus only worked miracles after he put their faith to the test. Faith is not a disposition of the heart but a fervent belief that takes root in action when tested. While we often pray for miracles, we do well to remember that such prayers are only granted after our faith, too, has been tested. However, what reward there is for those whose faith is steadfast.

Meditations from St. Therese

He whose Heart ever watcheth, taught me, that while for a soul whose faith equals but a tiny grain of mustard seed, he works miracles, in order that this faith which is so weak may be fortified; yet for His intimate friends, for His Mother, He did not work miracles until He had put their faith to the test. Did He not let Lazarus die though Martha and Mary had sent to tell Him that he was sick? At the marriage at Cana, the Blessed Virgin having asked Him to come to the assistance of the Master of the house, did He not reply that His hour was not yet come? But after the trial, what a recompense! Water changed to wine, Lazarus restored to life.

HIST. D'UNE AME, CH. VI

Additional Biblical Reflections: John 2:1-12; John 11; 1 Peter 1:7.

Prayer

Lord, how often we ask you for great things but lack the patience and faith to endure through the trial. Let us embrace times of testing in our lives, and that through such things, our faith might be made pure and genuine, and that we might be properly disposed to receive your good gifts. Amen.

DAY 9

Today, St. Therese reminds us of the promise of eternal life. While it sometimes seems that life struggles are never-ending, the only thing, in truth, that is eternal is God and His plans for us. Thus, even if we endure life-long hardships, we can take great comfort in knowing that with God, the best is yet to come.

Meditations from St. Therese

Life is passing, Eternity draws nigh; soon shall we live the very life of God. After having drunk deep at the fount of bitterness, our thirst will be quenched at the very source of all sweetness. Yes, the figure of this world passeth away, soon shall we see new heavens; a more radiant sun will brighten with its splendours, ethereal seas and infinite horizons . . . We shall no longer be prisoners in a land of exile, all will be at an end and with our Heavenly Spouse we shall sail o'er boundless waters: now our harps are hung upon the willows that border the rivers of Babylon, but in the day of our deliverance what harmonies will then be heard! With what joy shall we not make every chord of our instruments to vibrate! Today, we weep remembering Sion . . . how shall we sing the songs of the Lord in a strange land?

LETTER TO HER SISTER CÉLINE

Additional Biblical Reflections: Psalm 136; 1 Corinthians 7:31; 1 John 2:17.

Prayer

Thank you, Lord, for revealing your plan for our eternal future with you. Make us ever mindful of your promises and the splendor you have granted us for Jesus's sake, that we might not be overwhelmed by the cares of this world but endure them for what is yet to come. Amen.

DAY 10

Again, today, St. Therese reminds us of the splendor of the life to come. Here, she likens the humblest of us by worldly standards to martyrs, saints, doctors, and virgins. Even a simple child is valued as much as an Apostle or a patriarch. In an often unfair and unjust world, we can take comfort knowing that these injustices are temporary.

Meditations from St. Therese

Oh! What mysteries will be revealed to us later . . . How often have I thought that I perhaps owe all the graces showered upon me to the earnest prayer of a little soul whom I shall know only in Heaven. It is God's will that in this world by means of prayer Heavenly treasures should be imparted by souls one to another, so that when they reach the Fatherland they may love one another with a love born of gratitude, with an affection far, far exceeding the most ideal family affection upon earth. There, we shall meet with no indifferent looks, because all the Saints will be indebted to each other. No envious glances will be seen; the happiness of every one of the elect will be the happiness of all. With the Martyrs we shall be like the Martyrs; with the Doctors we shall be as the Doctors; with the Virgins, as the Virgins; and just as the members of a family are proud of one another, so shall we be of our brethren, without the least jealousy.

Who knows even if the joy we shall experience in beholding the glory of the great Saints, and knowing that by a secret dispensation of Providence we have contributed thereunto, who knows if this joy will not be as intense and sweeter perhaps, than the happiness they will themselves possess. And do you not think that on their side the great Saints, seeing what they owe to quite little souls, will love them with an incomparable love? Delightful and surprising will be the friendships found there—I am sure of it. The favoured companion of an Apostle or a great Doctor of the Church, will perhaps be a young shepherd lad; and a simple little child may be the intimate friend of a Patriarch. Oh! how I long to dwell in that Kingdom of Love . . .

COUNSELS AND REMINISCENCES

Additional Biblical Reflections: Psalm 89:14; Galatians 3:28; 2 Timothy 4:8.

Prayer

Lord, in this world, we are esteemed and often despised without just cause. However, your justice is wrapped in mercy. Let us take comfort in the fact that you heed the prayers of even sinners and the weak of faith, as you hear those of saints and martyrs. Let us pray "thy kingdom come" that your justice will prevail in this world and in the life to come. Amen.

DAY 11

One of the difficulties with doing good deeds is that the moment we do them, pride begins to well up within us, and we spoil it by allowing our piety to puff us up. Even worse, we often take additional pride in our appearance of piety before others. St. Therese offers us simple advice: Draw near to the heart of Christ and allow His deeds to flow through us without notice or care. Only in this way do deeds become truly "good deeds," when we find ourselves serving others not because we must, but because of who we are in Christ.

Meditations from St. Therese

Jesus made me understand that the true, the only glory is that which will last forever; that to attain to it we need not perform wonderful deeds, but rather, those hidden from the eyes of others and from self, so that the left hand knoweth not what the right hand doth.

HIST. D'UNE AME, CH. IV

Additional Biblical Reflections: Jeremiah 9:23-24; Ephesians 2:8-9; Matthew 6:1-3.

Prayer

Lord, you need not think about doing good to us but do so out of the abundance of your heart. Grant us hearts in your image that we might be spared from pride or boasting in our deeds, and instead, might serve all in love, and you alone might receive the glory. Amen.

DAY 12

Even the disciples lamented for a moment when Jesus told them he had to return to the Father. But Jesus declared it was necessary that he go away, and that he might send the Holy Spirit, a comforter, to guide us. The role of the Holy Spirit is to connect us with Christ in an ever-present way. While the Spirit is with us always, as Jesus himself promised, if we feel like we are lost or have wandered from the path, we need only contemplate the Gospels.

Meditations from St. Therese

Since Jesus has gone back to Heaven I can follow Him only by the path He has traced. Oh how luminous are His footprints—diffusing a divine sweetness. I have but to glance at the holy Gospels and immediately I inhale the fragrance of the life of Jesus, and I know aspire to be little and unknown.

LETTER TO HER SISTER CÉLINE

Additional Biblical Reflections: 1 Kings 18:12; Matthew 29:19-20; John 16:7.

Prayer

Lord, we do not always feel your presence in our lives. Nonetheless, you have promised you would be with us no less. Help us cling to your word of promise as we navigate our lives and that in all things, we might follow your path and give glory to you alone. Amen.

DAY 13

St. Therese recognizes that her example and words often cause struggle for the novices in her order, who would hope to follow her path. That her piety elicits a struggle in these young sisters is, to her, more than satisfying. This is an insight that comes from experience. Without trying, has the way we lived out our faith inadvertently challenged others and unsettled them? If so, St. Therese suggests that we should cherish it because God works through trials like these.

Meditations from St. Therese

With a simplicity that delights me my little Sisters, the novices, tell me of the interior combats I arouse in them, in what way they find me trying; they are no more embarrassed than if it were question of someone else, knowing that by acting thus, they greatly please me. Ah! truly it is more than a pleasure, it is a delicious feast which replenishes my soul with joy. How can a thing so disagreeable to nature give such happiness? Had I not experienced it I could not have believed it. One day when I had an ardent desire for humiliation, it happened that a young postulant so fully satisfied it, that the thought of Semei cursing David came to my mind and I repeated interiorly with the holy King: Yes, it is indeed the Lord who has commanded him to say all these things to me. Thus the good God takes care of me. He cannot always offer me the strength—giving bread of exterior humiliation, but from time to time He permits me to feast upon the crumbs that fall from the table of the children. How great is His Mercy!

HIST. D'UNE AME, CH. X

Additional Biblical Reflections: Jeremiah 22:3-5, Ecclesiastes 5:8, Romans 12:1-7.

Prayer

Lord, you showed us the art of suffering as you persisted through the cross. So, too, let us recognize that you work new life in us as we follow in your path and struggle with the principles of our faith. May these struggles be like the one who labors a field with toil, and the blessed struggles in our lives might bear the sweetest fruit. Amen.

DAY 14

Seeking the lowest of places rather than places of esteem is—St. Therese tells us—good for our souls. In lofty places, we tend to find vanity and "affliction of spirit," but when we humble ourselves, confess that we have "slipped" and cannot stand on our own, the Lord reaches out His hand to steady us. In His embrace, in the lowest place, is where we find holiness.

Meditations from St. Therese

The only thing not subject to be envied is the lowest place, it is therefore this lowest place alone which is without vanity and affliction of spirit. Still, the way of a man is not always in his power and sometimes we are surprised by a desire for that which glitters. Then, let us take our place humbly amongst the imperfect, deeming ourselves little souls whom the good God must sustain at each moment. As soon as He sees us truly convinced of our nothingness and we say to Him: My foot hath slipped: Thy mercy, O Lord, hath held me up, He stretches out His Hand to us; but if we will attempt to do something grand, even under pretext of zeal, He leaves us alone. It is enough therefore that we humble ourselves, and bear our imperfections with sweetness: there, for us, lies true sanctity.

COUNSELS AND REMINISCENCES

Additional Biblical Reflections: Jeremiah 10:23; Psalm 93; Luke 14:7-10.

Prayer

Your ways, Oh Lord, are not ours. You are not found in the lofty places but the lowest. Pray, Lord, that we have hearts to seek you in our humble estate, and thereby draw nearer to you and know you more. Amen.

DAY 15

God's grace and His gifts are all around us. Today, St. Therese bids us to consider the sweetness of a rose-tinted peach. This peach, she says, was made sweet for our sake. Our Lord does not only grant us gifts to sustain our lives in the world, but He gives us "lavish" things that we might enjoy the gift of life. So, as long as we recognize that these good things come from the great Giver, we need not be tempted to idolize the things of this world. Indeed, He desires that we would enjoy the gifts of the world all the more as we accept these things as His gifts.

Meditations from St. Therese

The most eloquent discourses would be incapable of inspiring one act of love without the grace that moves the heart. See a beautiful, rose-tinted peach, of so sweet a savor that no craft of confectioner could produce nectar like it. Is it for the peach itself that God has created this lovely color and delicate velvety surface? Is it for the sake of the peach that He has given it so delicious a flavor? No, it is for us; what alone belongs to it and forms the essence of its existence is its stone; it possesses nothing more. Thus is Jesus pleased to lavish His gifts on some of His creatures, that through them He may draw to Himself other souls; but in His mercy He humiliates them interiorly, and gently constrains them to recognize their nothingness and His Omnipotence. These sentiments form in them, as it were, a kernel of grace, which Jesus hastens to develop for that blessed day when clothed with a beauty, immortal, imperishable, they shall without danger have place at the Celestial banquet.

LETTER TO HER SISTER CÉLINE

Additional Biblical Reflections: Genesis 1:31; Psalm 40:5; Matthew 6:25-34.

Prayer

Lord, every good gift in this world comes from you. Yet too often, we seize what this world has to offer without giving thought to the fact that it was given to us by your hand. Let us always be thankful for the many blessings you have given us, and might we cherish our lives as your greatest gift and this world as the wondrous result of your handiwork. Amen.

DAY 16

It must have been embarrassing and frustrating for a professional fisherman to admit to Jesus that he had caught nothing through his night's labors. Still, when we recognize our humility and helplessness, our Lord is moved by compassion and goodness to act and intervene. In this way, Jesus demonstrates his character and goodness—the one who made all things also grants us all things. However, we must confess our helplessness and trust in His provision.

Meditations from St. Therese

The Apostles, without Jesus, labored long—a whole night—without taking any fish; their toil was pleasing to Him but He wished to show that He alone can give anything. He asked only an act of humility: "Children, have you any meat?" and St. Peter confesses his helplessness: "Lord we have labored all night and have taken nothing." It is enough! The Heart of Jesus is touched. Perhaps if the Apostle had taken a few little fishes the Divine Master would not have worked a miracle; but he had nothing, and so through God's power and goodness his nets were soon filled with great fishes. That is just our Lord's way. He gives as God, but He will have humility of heart.

LETTER TO HER SISTER CÉLINE

Additional Biblical Reflections: Psalm 116:6-16; Luke 5:5; John 21:5.

Prayer

Lord, your compassion exceeds even our needs and desire. Help us always to be mindful of our dependence on you and that we might not think ourselves self-sufficient but needy. For in such a poverty of spirit, your graces are magnified, and your name is glorified. Amen.

DAY 17

Meditations from St. Therese

A novice confided to her that she made no progress and felt quite discouraged. "Till the age of fourteen," said Therese, "I practiced virtue without feeling its sweetness. I wished for suffering but had no thought of finding my joy therein; that is a grace which has been granted me later. My soul was like a beautiful tree whose blossoms no sooner opened than they fell. "Offer to the good God the sacrifice of never gathering the fruits of your labors. If He so will that during your whole life you feel a repugnance to suffer and to be humiliated, if He permit that all the flowers of your desires and of your good-will fall to earth without fruit, be not troubled. At the moment of your death He will know well how to bring to perfection, in the twinkling of an eye, beautiful fruits on the tree of your soul. "We read in the Book of Ecclesiasticus: 'There is an inactive man that wanteth help, is very weak in ability, and full of poverty: yet the eye of God hath looked upon him for good, and hath lifted him up from his low estate, and hath exalted his head: and many have wondered at him and have glorified God.

'Trust in God, and stay in thy place. For it is easy in the eyes of God, on a sudden to make the poor man rich. The blessing of God maketh haste to reward the just, and in a swift hour His blessing beareth fruit!'"

COUNSELS AND REMINISCENCES

Additional Biblical Reflections: Exodus 18:23; Ecclesiasticus 11; 1 Timothy 6:12.

Prayer

Dear Lord, for you, a day is like a thousand years. However, we often treat every minute as if we had endured a thousand years in waiting. Grant us perseverance, Lord, and that the seeds of faith granted us might sprout and bear fruit in their due season. Let us not grow weary in waiting, but grant us the patience to see the fruit you have in store for us when we endure in faith. Amen.

DAY 18

Most of us do not like being corrected. If an unrepentant sinner challenges us, it makes sense that we might be ashamed. However, in truth, we rarely take the rebuke of even a just or righteous person well. In such moments, we should give thanks—rather than take offense— that the Lord has given us others who might lead us toward greater godliness.

Meditations from St. Therese

In a moment of temptation and combat a novice received this note: "The just man shall correct me in mercy and reprove me; but let not the oil of the sinner anoint my head. I cannot be corrected or tried except by the just, inasmuch as all my Sisters are pleasing to God. It is less bitter to be reproved by a sinner than by the just; but through compassion for sinners, to obtain their conversion, I pray Thee, O my God, that I may be bruised by the just souls who are round about me. Again, I beg that the oil of praise, so sweet to nature, anoint not my head, that is to say, enervate not my mind, by making me believe that I possess virtues which I have only with difficulty practiced several times.

"O my Jesus! Thy Name is as oil poured out; it is in this divine perfume that I wish to be wholly bathed, far away from the notice of creatures."

COUNSELS AND REMINISCENCES

Additional Biblical Reflections: Proverbs 9:8; Psalm 140; Luke 17:3-4.

Prayer

Lord, send us godly men and women who are willing to speak the truth to us in love. Let us not rear back in wounded pride when corrected but embrace a rebuke with gratitude. You have not sent us fellow believers to coddle us in our sin but to speak a harsh word, out of love, when warranted. Let us respond with appropriate penitence when called to account and give thanks that you have provided others to steer us toward godliness. Amen.

DAY 19

One of the trappings of spiritual progress is arrogance. Today, St. Therese reminds us that honors are always dangerous, and men's praises can be poison. Still, when we progress in piety, others will notice and praise us for it. In such instances, we dare never accept these praises as if they are due, but always direct such praises to the Lord who sanctifies us.

Meditations from St. Therese

"GOD has a special love for you," remarked a young Sister, "since to you He entrusts other souls." "That does not add anything to me, and I am only really just what I am in God's sight . . . It does not follow that He loves me more, because He wills that I should be His interpreter to you; rather, He makes me your little servant. It is for you and not for me that He has given me the charms and virtues apparent to you. "Often I compare myself to a little bowl which God fills with good things of every kind. All the kittens come to it to take their share, and sometimes there is a contest as to which shall have most. But the Child Jesus is there, keeping watch: 'I am very willing that you drink from my little bowl' saith He, 'but take care lest you overturn it and break it.' "Truth to tell, the danger is not great, because I am placed on the ground. It is otherwise with Prioresses: they, being set on tables run many more risks. Honors are always dangerous. "Oh! how poisonous the praises served up day by day to those who hold high places.

What baneful incense! And how necessary it is that the soul be detached from self, that so she may escape unharmed."

COUNSELS AND REMINISCENCES

Additional Biblical Reflections: 1 Samuel 16:7; John 5:44; Galatians 1:10.

Prayer

Lord, help us always to be mindful that any progress we have experienced in our walk toward you has come through your efforts in our hearts. Let us not become prideful when others observe our progress and, even more, let us not become content or imagine that we have attained the fullness of spiritual life. Rather, let us always give you the glory that we might not inadvertently wander from your path. Amen.

DAY 20

The esteem of other people is highly prized in the world. Without a good name, one can hardly experience success, and a name that has been ill-considered can cause great hardship. But for the Lord, we all have one name—the name in which we were Baptized—and what we seek should not be the greatness of our names but the consolation of our souls, wherein we find the great name of Christ sealed upon us.

Meditations from St. Therese

Far from dazzling me all the titles of nobility appear to me but empty vanity. I have understood those words of the Imitation: "Be not solicitous for the shadow of a great name." I have understood that true greatness is found not in the name but in the soul. The Prophet tells us that the Lord God shall call His servants by another name; and we read in St. John: "To him that overcometh, I will give . . . a white counter, and in the counter a new name written, which no man knoweth but he that receiveth." It is in Heaven, therefore, that we shall know our titles of nobility. Then shall each one receive from God the praise that he merits, and he who upon earth will have made choice of being the poorest and the most unknown for love of our Lord, he will be the first, the noblest and the richest.

HIST. D'UNE AME, CH. VI

Additional Biblical Reflections: Isaiah 65:15; 1 Corinthians 4:5.

Prayer

Dear Lord, you have placed your triune name upon each of us and thereby called us your children. Let us seek no glory in our own names nor let the esteem or ill repute of our name determine our worth. Rather, let us be ever mindful that our worth is measured in the cost you paid for our souls. Amen.

DAY 21

In today's meditation, St. Therese shares a moment from her childhood wherein she grew temporarily jealous of her sister. However, as such sentiments boiled up within her, she decided to remain silent and instead turned to Jesus. Yet here, she teaches us that taming the tongue when our pride is wounded can direct us to ponder the Lord, for when we speak up to defend ourselves, we often give voice to our envy and arrogance.

Meditations from St. Therese

I was ten years old the day that my Father told Céline he was going to let her have lessons in painting; I was by, and envied her. Then Papa said to me: "And you, my little queen, would it give you pleasure too to learn drawing?" I was just going to respond with a very gladsome yes, when Marie made the remark that I had not the same taste for it as Céline. At once she gained the day; and I, thinking that here was a good opportunity of offering a grand sacrifice to Jesus, said not a word. So eager was my desire to learn drawing that now I still wonder how I had the fortitude to remain silent.

HIST. D'UNE AME, CH. VIII

Additional Biblical Reflections: Romans 12:6-8; 1 Corinthians 12:12-27; James 3:1-12.

Prayer

Lord, you often speak to us in silence. Let us be slow to speak when we feel slighted or wounded, and that rather than compound our problems, we might find peace in your presence. In Jesus's name. Amen.

DAY 22

Many of us live in fear of bad things happening. We have often grown jaded by injustices and trials we have suffered, and we worry that these things might compound upon us in our lives. In today's meditation, St. Therese shows how—as she has drawn closer to Jesus, who taught us how to suffer—we might look toward a day's troubles with a different attitude entirely.

Meditations from St. Therese

In the world, on awakening in the morning I used to think over what would probably occur either pleasing or vexatious during the day; and if I foresaw only trying events I arose dispirited. Now it is quite the other way: I think of the difficulties and the sufferings that await me, and I rise the more joyous and full of courage the more I foresee opportunities of proving my love for Jesus, and earning the living of my children—seeing that I am the mother of souls. Then I kiss my crucifix and lay it tenderly on the pillow while I dress, and I say to Him: "My Jesus, Thou hast worked enough and wept enough during the three-and-thirty years of Thy life on this poor earth. Take now Thy rest . . . My turn it is to suffer and to fight."

COUNSELS AND REMINISCENCES

Additional Biblical Reflections: Habakkuk 3:17-19; Matthew 5:12; Hebrews 12:2.

Prayer

Lord, for the joy set before you, you endured the cross and scorned its shame. Set your cross always before our eyes so that every morning when we rise, it might be as a little resurrection with victory over the struggles that the world might throw upon us. In Jesus's name. Amen.

DAY 23

It is not always the big trials and tribulations that vex us the most. Sometimes, the small annoyances that grate upon us until we find ourselves reacting in an ungodly way. In a moment of candor, St. Therese reflects how another sister with a simple habit caused her such an annoyance that she found herself on the brink of sin. However, rather than show her irritation, she took the opportunity to accept it as an occasion to learn patience and the love of another.

Meditations from St. Therese

At prayer I was for a long time near a Sister who used to handle incessantly either her Rosary-beads or some other thing; perhaps none heard it but myself, for my hearing is extremely acute, but I cannot say how it tormented me! I should have liked to turn my head and look at the culprit so as to make her stop that noise: however in my heart I knew it was better to bear it patiently, for the love of God in the first place, and also to avoid giving pain. I kept quiet therefore, but was sometimes worked up to fever-heat and obliged to make simply a prayer of endurance. Finally I sought out the means of suffering with peace and joy, at least in my innermost soul; I tried to like the teasing little noise. Instead of endeavoring not to hear it—a thing impossible—I listened with fixed attention as if it had been a delightful concert; and my prayer, which was not the prayer of quiet, passed in offering this concert to Jesus. Another time I was in the laundry opposite a Sister who while washing handkerchiefs splashed me every minute with dirty water. My first impulse was to draw back and wipe my face, so as to show her who besprinkled me in that fashion, that she would oblige me by working more quietly; but I reflected immediately that it was very foolish to refuse treasures so generously offered me, and I took good care not to show my annoyance. On the contrary, I made such successful efforts to wish for a plentiful splashing of dirty water, that at the end of half an hour I had really acquired a taste for this new sort of aspersion, and I determined to come again as often as possible to a place where happily such riches could be had gratuitously.

HIST. D'UNE AME, CH. X

Additional Biblical Reflections:

Prayer

Lord, let us not become perplexed by the little annoyances of this life. Rather, show us the opportunity to grow, and show your love when such things vex us that we might be spared from sin and grow deeper in intimacy with you. Amen.

DAY 24

Even when we know we are guilty of sin, St. Therese urges that we should take refuge in the Lord's embrace, sure of his love and character. Despair is not a cure for sin in itself. In despair, we often fail to see the Father's loving gaze as He longs to take us into His arms. Out of desolation, we should learn to embrace the Lord and rest in His embrace.

Meditations from St. Therese

I want to make you understand by a very simple comparison how much Jesus loves souls, even the imperfect, who trust in Him. Suppose the father of two wayward and disobedient children, coming to punish them, sees one tremble and draw away from him in terror; while the other, on the contrary, throwing himself into his arms, says he is sorry, promises to be good henceforward and begs for a kiss as punishment. Do you think the delighted father will withstand the filial confidence of this child? He knows nevertheless that his son will fall again many a time into the same faults, but he is disposed to pardon him always, if always there be an appeal to his heart. I say nothing of the other child: you must understand that his father cannot love him as much or treat him with the same indulgence.

LETTER TO HER MISSIONARY "BROTHERS"

Additional Biblical Reflections: Joel 2:12-13; Luke 15:11-32; 1 John 4:10.

Prayer

Lord, you know we are prone to fall and sin, yet you stand very willing to embrace us when we return to you. Let us now not wallow in unnecessary despair, but in Godly penitence rest in your embrace and know your steadfast love, for you are gracious and merciful. Amen.

DAY 25

The Lord is overjoyed—as the father of the prodigal—when we return to Him after we sin. Too many people, after falling into sin, wallow in their guilt for a season. This accomplishes nothing because we cannot progress in our piety if we separate ourselves from God. Of course, we are unworthy of His love, but that has always been the case. Who are we to tell God that He should not embrace us when He desires to?

Meditations from St. Therese

Truly the Heart of Jesus is more grieved by the thousand little imperfections of His friends than by even grave faults of His enemies. But it seems to me that it is only when His own chosen ones make a habit of these infidelities, and do not ask His pardon, that He can say: "These wounds which you see in the midst of My Hands: with these was I wounded in the house of them that loved Me." For those who love Him and who come after each little fault and throw themselves into His arms, begging His forgiveness, the Heart of Jesus thrills with joy. He says to His Angels what the father of the prodigal son said to His servants: "Put a ring on his finger and let us rejoice." Oh! the goodness and the merciful love of the Heart of Jesus, how little is it known! True it is, that to share in these treasures we must humble ourselves, must acknowledge our nothingness, and that is what many souls are unwilling to do.

LETTER TO HER MISSIONARY "BROTHERS"

Additional Biblical Reflections: Zechariah 13:6; Luke 15:22.

Prayer

Lord, you rejoice when we return to you. Let us learn to come to you whenever we stumble, and that you might put us back on our feet again and restore us to the path of righteousness. In Jesus's name. Amen.

DAY 26

When we perceive holy men and women, we often imagine that these are people who have never fallen into mortal sin. St. Therese dispels this notion in today's meditation. Those who are made holy in piety are not so because they have been shielded from sin, but because when they have sinned, they have quickly turned to the Lord.

Meditations from St. Therese

It is not because I have been shielded from mortal sin that I lift up my heart to God in trust and love. I feel that even if there lay upon my conscience all the crimes one could commit I should lose nothing of my confidence. Brokenhearted with compunction I would go and throw myself into the arms of my Savior. I know that He cherished the Prodigal Son, I have heard His words to Mary Magdalene, to the adulteress, to the Samaritan woman. No one could frighten me, for I know what to believe concerning His Mercy and His Love. I know that in one moment all that multitude of sins would disappear—as a drop of water cast into a red-hot furnace. It is related in the Lives of the Fathers of the Desert that one of them converted a public sinner whose misdeeds scandalized the whole country. Touched by grace this sinful woman was following the saint into the desert, there to do rigorous penance, when, on the first night of her journey, before she had even reached the place of her retreat, the bonds of life were broken by the impetuosity of her loving contrition. The holy hermit at the same moment saw her soul borne by Angels into the Bosom of God. That is truly a striking instance of what I want to express, but one cannot put these things into words.

HIST. D'UNE AME, CH. XI

Additional Biblical Reflections: Matthew 25:40, Philippians 2:4-8, 1 John 3:17.

Prayer

Lord, you know our hearts, including our weaknesses. You know when we fall and even when we are likely to fail. Yet you still bear with us in patience. Let us learn that the path to holiness is not in being sheltered from sin or the absence of failings, but in our willingness to cast our sins upon your Son, who bore them willingly for our sake. Amen.

DAY 27

In today's meditation, St. Therese uses the metaphor of a "Bank of Love," an unending deposit of good favor that God has stored up for us that we might draw upon in moments when we are discouraged. When we find ourselves lacking faith or acting out of character with what God would desire for us, we must draw upon that Bank of Love and find the strength to correct our path.

Meditations from St. Therese

I am not always faithful, but I am never discouraged; I leave myself wholly in the arms of our Divine Lord; He teaches me to draw profit from all—both good and ill that He finds in me. He teaches me to speculate in the Bank of Love, or rather it is He who acts for me without telling me how He goes to work, that is His affair and not mine; my part is complete surrender, reserving nothing to myself, not even the gratification of knowing how my credit stands with the Bank.

LETTER TO HER SISTER CÉLINE

Additional Biblical Reflections: Mark 7:6, Ephesians:1-33, 2 Thessalonians 3:6.

Prayer

Lord, your love for us is abundant. Let us never imagine that your love for us has run thin. Rather, teach us to always return to your Bank of Love when we find ourselves going astray and that we might once again be shown the path of holiness. Amen.

DAY 28

Anxiety is not only a common experience but, in today's word, a diagnosable condition. Fearing for our future, worried about what might happen, can paralyze us in the present. In today's meditation, St. Therese bids us neither to wallow in the past nor to anticipate the future. Rather, we must always find God where we are in the moment.

Meditations from St. Therese

You are quite wrong to think of sorrows that the future may bring; it is, as it were, intermeddling with Divine Providence. We who run in the way of Love must never torment ourselves about anything. If I did not suffer minute by minute, it would be impossible for me to be patient; but I see only the present moment, I forget the past and I take good care not to anticipate the future. If we grow disheartened, if sometimes we despair, it is because we have been dwelling on the past or the future.

HIST. D'UNE AME, CH. XII

Additional Biblical Reflections: Isaiah 35:4; Luke 12:22; 1 John 4:18.

Prayer

Lord, you are an ever-present God who redeems our past and knows our future. Let us not grow weary or anxious by worrying about the future, lest such worry causes us to sin today. Instead, let us take comfort in your presence in the present and move through each moment in godliness. Amen.

DAY 29

While the Lord will embrace us when we fall, we should also take care to note that the Lord has promised not to tempt us beyond what we can bear. The Lord has walked the path before us—like the doctor in the story St. Therese tells us in today's meditation—and cleared away any stones that might be too great for us. In this, we should have confidence that the Lord knows whatever temptations that remain we can overcome with his aid.

Meditations from St. Therese

I understand well that our Lord knew I was too weak to be exposed to temptation; without doubt I should have been wholly destroyed had I been dazzled by the deceitful glamour of the love of creatures; but never has it shone before my eyes. There, where strong souls find joy, and through fidelity detach themselves from it, I have found only affliction. Where then is my merit in not being given up to these fragile attachments, since it is only by a gracious effect of God's mercy that I was preserved from it? Without Him, I recognize that I might have fallen as low as St. Magdalene; and that word of deep meaning spoken by the Divine Master to Simon the Pharisee, re-echoes with great sweetness in my soul. Yes, I know it: "To whom less is forgiven, he loveth less." But I also know that Jesus has forgiven more to me than to St. Magdalene. Ah, how I wish I could express what I feel. Here at least is an example which will in some measure convey my thought.

Suppose the son of a skilful doctor is tripped by a stone in his path, which causes him to fall and fracture a limb. His father comes in haste, lifts him up lovingly and attends to his injuries, employing therein all the resources of his art; and the boy, very soon completely cured, testifies his gratitude. This child has certainly good reason to love so kind a father; but here is another supposition.

The father having learnt that there lies in his son's way a dangerous stone, sets out beforehand and removes it unseen by anyone. His son, the object of this tender forethought, unaware of the misfortune from which he has been preserved by the father's hand, will of course show no gratitude, and will love him less than if he had cured him of a grievous wound. But should he come to know all, will he not love him still more? Well—I am this child, the object of the preventing love of a Father Who sent His Son not to redeem the just but sinners. He wills that I should love Him because He has forgiven me, not much, but everything. Without waiting for me to love Him much, like St. Mary Magdalene, He has made me to know how He had loved me with a preventing and ineffable love, in order that I may now love Him even unto folly!

HIST. D'UNE AME, CH. IV

Additional Biblical Reflections: 1 Corinthians 10:13; Luke 5:32, 7:47.

Prayer

Lord, you care for us at every step of life. We thank you for going ahead of us and ensuring that no temptation greater than what we can handle has befallen us. Let us face temptation with confidence, and if we endure it with you, we will not fail. In Jesus's name. Amen.

DAY 30

St. Therese speaks of God as the great "fulcrum" upon which we, as His saints, can uplift the world. Let us learn not to toil with anxiety to please the Lord, like Marth, but to do whatever we have been called to do with confidence, like Mary.

Meditations from St. Therese

Souls thus on fire cannot rest inactive. They may sit at the feet of Jesus, like Saint Mary Magdalene, listening to His sweet and ardent words; but, while seeming to give nothing, they do give far more than Martha who troubles herself with many things. It is not however of Martha's labors that Jesus disapproves, but only her too great anxiety; to this very same work His Blessed Mother humbly submitted herself, when she had to prepare the repasts for the Holy Family. All the Saints have understood this, and more especially perhaps those who have enlightened the world with the luminous teaching of the Gospel. Was it not from prayer that Saint Paul, Saint Augustine, Saint Thomas of Aquin, Saint John of the Cross, Saint Teresa and so many other friends of God drew that wondrous science which enraptures the greatest intellects? Archimedes said: "Give me a lever and a fulcrum, and I will raise the world." What he was unable to obtain because his request had but a material end and was not addressed to God, the Saints have obtained in full measure. For fulcrum, the Almighty has given them Himself, Himself alone! for lever, prayer, which enkindles the fire of love;

and thus it is that they have uplifted the world, thus it is that saints still militant, uplift it, and will uplift it till the end of time.

HIST. D'UNE AME, CH. XI

Additional Biblical Reflections: Luke 10:41.

Prayer

Lord, in you, is only wisdom, but in your love, you bear with our foolishness. Help us see the great comfort and peace that comes with your presence, and may your peace cast out all anxiety and fear. On the fulcrum of your gift of love, let us all uplift the world that you might be glorified throughout creation. Amen.